IAN McALLISTER & NICHOLAS READ

A WHALE'S WORLD

ORCA BOOK PUBLISHERS

Library and Archives Canada Cataloguing in Publication

McAllister, Ian, 1969–, author, photographer
A whale's world / Ian McAllister, Nicholas Read.
(My Great Bear Rainforest)

Issued in print and electronic formats.
ISBN 978-1-4598-1273-4 (hardcover).—ISBN 978-1-4598-1274-1 (pdf).—
ISBN 978-1-4598-1275-8 (epub)

1. Killer whale—British Columbia—Pacific Coast—Juvenile literature.
2. Pacific Coast (B.C.)—Juvenile literature. 3. Great Bear Rainforest
(B.C.)—Juvenile literature. 4. Rain forest ecology—British
Columbia—Juvenile literature. 5. Coastal ecology—British Columbia—
Juvenile literature.

I. Read, Nicholas, 1956–, author II. Title.
III. Series: McAllister, Ian, 1969– .
My Great Bear Rainforest.

QL737.C432M28 2018   j599.53'609711   C2017-907843-7
                           C2017-907844-5

Summary: This nonfiction picture book is part of the My Great Bear
Rainforest series. Stunning photographs depict a pod of orcas as they roam
the waters of the Great Bear Sea, hunting for their next meal.

First published in the United States, 2018
Library of Congress Control Number: 2018933699

*Orca Book Publishers is dedicated to preserving the environment and has
printed this book on Forest Stewardship Council® certified paper.*

Orca Book Publishers gratefully acknowledges the support for
its publishing programs provided by the following agencies:
the Government of Canada through the Canada Book Fund and the
Canada Council for the Arts, and the Province of British Columbia
through the BC Arts Council and the Book Publishing Tax Credit.

Cover and interior images by Ian McAllister
Edited by Sarah N. Harvey
Design by Rachel Page
Image management by Deirdre Leowinata

About the photographs:
All of the images in this book are of wild animals in wild circumstances.
No digital manipulation or other alterations have taken place.

ORCA BOOK PUBLISHERS
orcabook.com

Printed and bound in Canada.

21 20 19 18 • 4 3 2 1

It's a beautiful day on the Great Bear Sea. There's barely any wind, so there are hardly any waves. You can see for miles in every direction. You can see the skyscraper trees of the Great Bear Rainforest. You can see the barnacle-laden rocks on shore. And you can see the sea itself, spreading out like a big blue blanket.

A small pod of orcas is searching for food. One of them lifts the top third of her body out of the water and holds it there. It's a move called spy-hopping, and it lets the orca see what's going on above the water and on land. She looks like a periscope.

The orca is looking for a seal or sea lion that her pod can share for lunch. But there are none around. Instead she sees a grizzly bear on the seashore, upending rocks and logs as he looks for mussels, barnacles and crabs. You may not think grizzly bears eat seafood, but in the Great Bear Rainforest they love it.

The orca also sees a black bear hiding in the bushes. Black bears are nervous around grizzlies because they are so much smaller. This one doesn't want to draw any attention to himself while the grizzly is around. He's happy to wait till the grizzly finishes his snack before he starts his own beachcombing.

Farther down the beach, the orca notices a wolf digging in the sand for clams. He looks just like a dog with his front paws spinning like a wheel.

The orca also sees another, much bigger whale. Orcas can grow to be the size of a stretch limousine. But this whale, called a fin whale, is as big as a bus. Orcas are black and white, but the fin whale is bluish gray. And unlike the orcas, he's not looking for seals or sea lions. Despite being so huge, fin whales eat creatures called plankton and krill, which are so tiny you have to use a microscope to see them.

The orca decides to take a look around under the waves. Maybe she'll see a seal or sea lion swimming by that she can chase. But all she sees are fish. More than three hundred kinds of fish live in the Great Bear Sea, ranging from the crayon-sized northern anchovy to the lightning-fast blue shark, a rare species that can grow as long as a police car.

There are five species of salmon in the Great Bear Sea, and each one is vitally important to the health of the rainforest. That's because they return to the forest's rivers when their time in the sea is done, where they become food for bears, wolves and eagles. Any parts of the fish that aren't eaten feed the soil, which in turn feeds the trees.

The orca also spots several schools of herring. In the spring, when herring lay eggs in seaweed or on rocks, gulls, eagles, cormorants and loons swoop out of the sky to attack them. Then the eggs are eaten by bears, wolves and gray whales. Any surviving eggs become silvery fish, which may get eaten by other fish, marine mammals and people.

Three very small species of fish—sand lance, sardine and eulachon—are in the orca's sight lines too. Despite their size—no bigger than your pointer finger—they are hugely important to the Great Bear Sea because so many other types of fish—such as herring, cod, pollock, halibut, sturgeon, dogfish and salmon—eat them. That's the way of the ocean. One fish always eats another.

Looking down, the orca spots a sea creature that isn't a whale or a fish. It's a Pacific octopus, the largest octopus in the world. Pacific octopuses are as long as alligators. They're also very smart. They've even been known to use primitive tools.

The orca is getting frustrated. Where are all the seals and sea lions? How will she and her pod fill their bellies if they don't find something to eat? She decides to look above the water again. Maybe she'll spy a seal swimming toward a sun-warmed rock. Then she and her pod can capture it.

All she sees are birds. Bald eagles circle over the beach and perch in the high branches of the forest's biggest cedars and firs. They are proud-looking birds with golden beaks and snow-white cowls.

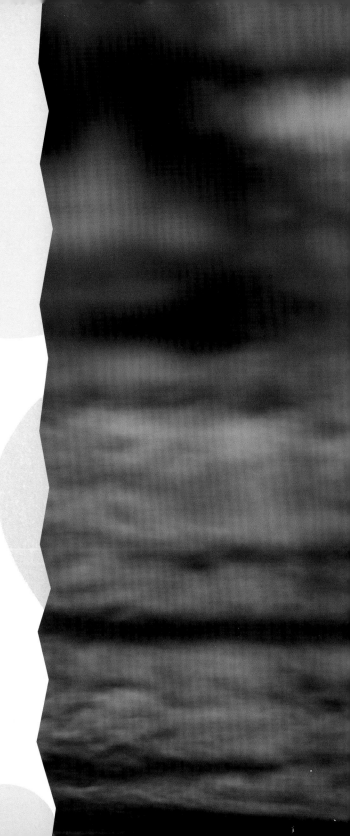

Eagles and a lot of other birds who live at the edge of the Great Bear Sea eat fish and other types of seafood. Sometimes seagulls fly with clamshells in their beaks and drop them on flat rocks to smash them open. That way they can get at the delicious, squishy animal inside.

Puffins have bright-orange bills, white masks and long golden feathers cascading down the backs of their heads. They also have orangey-red webbed feet. Unlike other birds, a puffin can hold several fish in its beak at once. When a puffin goes fishing, it can fly back to shore with a bigger catch in its mouth.

Spinning her body away from the land, the orca sees a dolphin frolicking in the distance. Pacific white-sided dolphins love to jump for the sheer joy of it. They also ride boats' bow waves and follow in their wakes. And because dolphins are so curious, they'll travel miles to check out a boat cruising in their territory.

But none of this is of interest to the orca and her pod, who are getting very hungry. Usually the Great Bear Sea is full of harbor seals, which are about as big as a stuffed hockey bag. But today they are all hiding.

Orcas also hunt Steller sea lions, which can weigh as much as a small car and grow as long as a bison. That's a big meal. They're called sea lions because they roar like land lions. And they walk on land using all four flippers.

But there are no sea lions around either. So
the orcas decide to travel farther down the coast to
where the hunting may be better.

As they swim, they stay in fairly shallow water. Below them are sea stars. Some are big, and some are small. The sunflower sea star is as big as an umbrella and has twenty-four legs that extend from its center like rays.

The orcas also swim past hundreds of sea urchins. *Urchin* is a very old word for "hedgehog," which is what urchins look like. Sea urchins can be black, green, olive, brown, purple, blue or red. And even though sea urchins are spiny, sea otters, sea stars, eels, fish and even humans eat them.

At one point the orcas enter a kelp forest. Among the many animals and birds that use kelp forests for protection and feeding are seals, sea lions, sea otters, gulls, great blue herons, cormorants and whales. But today only one seal is sighted, and it quickly hides from the orcas.

So the orcas keep swimming south. In no time, they've vanished. Not so much as a ripple remains.

This is when a harbor seal feels safe enough to emerge from her hiding spot in the kelp bed and haul herself onto a rock. She's been waiting for the orcas to disappear to show herself. Now she can relax on the rock and enjoy the calm sea. It's a good day to be alive on the Great Bear Sea.

Also in the MY GREAT BEAR RAINFOREST series

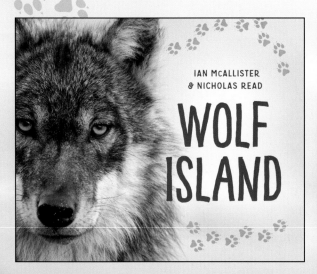

IAN McALLISTER
& NICHOLAS READ

WOLF ISLAND

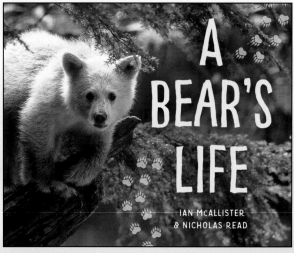

A BEAR'S LIFE

IAN McALLISTER
& NICHOLAS READ

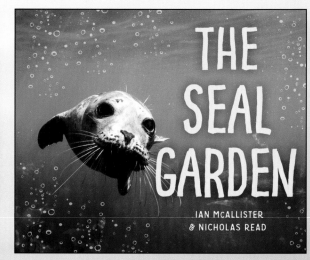

THE SEAL GARDEN

IAN McALLISTER
& NICHOLAS READ

"Read together, these books...provide opportunities for readers to compare and contrast the habits, homes and personalities of some of their favourite animals in a highly engaging and informative way. Full of universal themes...the books in the My Great Bear Rainforest series will delight readers of all interests and abilities."

—*Canadian Children's Booknews*

For more information about this spectacular place and Ian McAllister's stunning photography, please visit greatbearbooks.com or pacificwild.org.